# Getting to Know
## Spain

illustrated by
DON LAMBO

# Getting to know

# Spain

## by Dee Day

FREDERICK MULLER LIMITED                    LONDON

## ACKNOWLEDGMENTS

The author wishes to acknowledge the assistance and hospitality of Direccion General del Turismo in all its offices in Spain, the Spanish State Tourist Department in New York, and Iberia Air Lines of Spain, without whose co-operation the gathering of much of the material and the personal experience reflected in this book would have been impossible. A majority of the pictures were drawn from photographs by Herb Kratovil, taken especially for this book.

Dee Day

Printed in Great Britain by Jarrold & Sons Ltd, Norwich

For My Parents

YOU PROBABLY KNOW that it was in Spain, during the reign of Queen Isabella, in the fifteenth century, that Christopher Columbus first had the strange new idea that he could sail westward from the Spanish coast to reach the Far East. He came from Italy to Spain to tell people about his idea, and everybody he met thought he was mad because they knew, or thought they knew, that the northern corner of Spain, jutting out into the Atlantic, was the very end of the world. Even the most daring sailors and fishermen wouldn't go very far from that shore for fear they would drop over the rim into nothingness.

But Queen Isabella didn't think Columbus was mad. She took time to listen to him and decided she wanted to help him. She didn't have any money to buy ships for his expedition, so she ordered a little fishing village, Palos, to build three ships as a way of paying a fine they owed her. The fishermen of Palos knew how to build good, sturdy sailing vessels, and they soon had the three ships ready for Columbus and his brave sailors.

That is why, in August of 1492, the daring expedition started from this little Spanish village. What a sight! Three little ships, the *Niña* (Small Girl), the *Pinta* (Spotted), and the *Santa Maria* (named in honour of the Virgin Mary) cast off from the wharf of Palos. Flags fluttered in the breeze as the sails billowed out from the masts. All the villagers were lined up on the shore to pray and to cheer, and the bells in the church rang as Columbus and his crew sailed off "the rim" to the west in search of wealth and glory for Spain!

Many Spanish explorers followed Columbus to the New World,

and even sailed all the way around the world, west to east, but the Spanish people today are mostly "stay-at-homes". Sometimes they leave home for a little while to make money, like the Spanish

shepherds who are so good at handling flocks of sheep that ranchers in America pay them a lot of money to go and work for them. But those who leave always go back to their beloved land as soon as they have earned what they need.

If you were to meet a Spanish person, you would find that he would be interested in Britain and other countries, but he couldn't

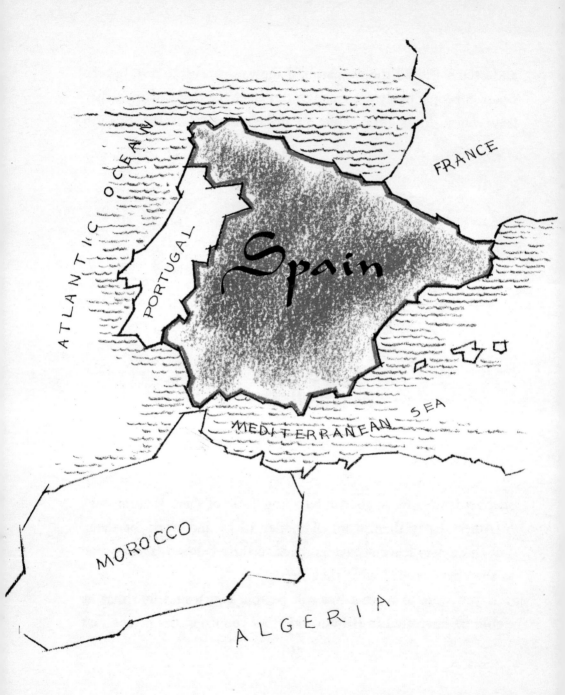

imagine living the rest of his life anywhere except in Spain. "Why should I ever live anywhere else?" he would ask you. "Everything beautiful and good in life is right here." He would feel this way even though he might be very poor and might even have to leave for a little while, like the shepherds. To him, the important things in life are his family, his friends, his church and his country.

His country is a large, squarish, mountainous land at the southwesternmost tip of Europe. To the north, over the tall wall of the Pyrenees Mountains, is France. To the west is Portugal and the Atlantic Ocean, and to the east is the Mediterranean Sea. Spain has more sea-coast than any other country on the mainland of Europe, and more mountains than any except Switzerland. Spain and Portugal together make up what is called the Iberian Peninsula. It is named after the Iberian people who came there from North Africa almost 5,000 years ago and settled down to become the ancestors of the Spanish people.

If you were to stand at the bottom of the Iberian Peninsula, on a hill overlooking a town called Algeciras, you could look right into Africa, only twelve miles away. You would also see

Gibraltar, which belongs to Britain and is a giant rock rising out of the sea and turned into a fort to guard the narrow passage between the Atlantic Ocean and the Mediterranean Sea. This passage is the Strait of Gibraltar, and all ships must go through it to get from the sea to the ocean.

In this mountainous country between two seas, more babies are born every day than in any other country in Europe.

There are 29 million people in Spain already, and it is the third largest country in Europe. And because their mountains shut different parts of the country away from each other, there are many differences in ways of living among the 29 million Spaniards. There are 15 different regions in Spain, and each one has a different way of dressing, different music and dances, different ways of cooking food, a different sort of house to live in, and even different ways of speaking. Sometimes you will meet a Spaniard who has never been out of his own region, or even away from his own village, because the mountains make it very difficult to travel

when your way of getting around is on your own two feet or in a little cart pulled by a small burro or donkey.

Another reason for the many different ways of living is that Spain is a very old country which has been invaded many times by other countries. These countries were jealous of the beauty and wealth of Spain and wanted to get it for themselves. For hundreds of years the Spanish people were always fighting to protect their beloved homeland against invading armies.

The Iberians themselves were invaders, because they weren't the first people who lived in Spain. We don't even know the

names of those very first people who lived there when most of Europe was covered with ice. We only know that they lived in caves and hunted wild animals, because some of their caves have been discovered and the walls are covered with bright drawings of the animals these people hunted—bison, deer, wild horses and wild boars.

After the Iberians came the Celts, Greeks, Phoenicians, Carthaginians and Romans. From Rome, Spain took her language, her system of laws, and her Church. There were once more than 80 Roman cities in Spain, with roads and bridges and walls which

were built so well that they are still used by Spanish people today. In the city of Segovia, the Romans built an aqueduct to bring drinking water into the town from the nearby mountains, and this aqueduct still brings water to the people of Segovia.

The Romans liked Spain so much they stayed 500 years, but finally barbaric tribes from central Europe drove them out. A short time later, these tribes were conquered by Moors from North Africa. The Moors brought many new ways to the Spanish people. They spoke the Arabic language, and worshipped Mohammed instead of Christ, in churches called mosques. They taught the Spanish people algebra and the science of astronomy; they introduced a new kind of poetry, music and dancing. They brought many new kinds of trees and flowers to Spain, like the date palm, the orange and the pomegranate, and taught the people how to grow them with an irrigation system which is still in use today. Many little Spanish boys learn how to run it, so that they can help their fathers and mothers.

The Moors built many mosques and palaces in Spain which are still in use, and they look like buildings from Arabian fairy tales. These Moorish buildings have their rooms built around open courtyards, called patios, where orange and lemon trees and many bright flowers grow, and fountains splash in the sun-

shine. The rooms have many pillars to support the ceiling, and all the pillars and arches and ceilings are beautifully carved. The Moors could carve hard stone so that it looks like delicate lace, and this is what gives their buildings such a fairy-tale look.

The Spanish Christians, however, didn't like the Moors, and during all the 800 years the Moors ruled Spain, the Christians were fighting to drive them out. Finally, Queen Isabella and her husband, King Ferdinand, led their Christian army to victory against the last Moorish stronghold, Granada. Because of this victory, Queen Isabella did not have to worry about fighting for a while, and she was able to help Columbus.

When Columbus discovered America on October 12, 1492, he began Spain's most exciting period of history. The next century after Columbus was called the Age of the Conquistadores. Conquistadores were adventurers who set out to find and conquer new lands for Spain in the New World which Columbus had discovered. Many of their conquests later became part of the United States. For instance, De Soto claimed the Mississippi River and all the rivers that run into it, as well as part of the land that is now the American south-west. Ponce de Leon, looking for a magic fountain that would keep people young for ever, discovered Florida and claimed for Spain the land that is now the American south-east. Cortez, who had conquered Mexico for Spain and had sent millions of pounds' worth of gold and jewels back to his homeland, also travelled through the south-west and as far north as Colorado. The great Pacific Ocean, which washes the western coast of both North and South America, was discovered by a Spaniard named Balboa. One Spanish sailor, Juan Sebastian Elcano, was the very first man to sail all the way around the world.

The Conquistadores sent back a huge treasure of gold, silver, copper and jewels to Spain, and more than paid Queen Isabella and her family for her faith in Columbus. In fact, Spain became one of the most important countries in Europe. Her queens and kings and princesses married rulers of other countries so that soon, in addition to being very rich and owning many countries across the ocean, Spain owned much of Europe too. Only England had stood up against the Spanish power. So in 1588, Spain sent a great fleet of warships, called the Armada, to challenge England, but, as you know, it suffered a disastrous defeat.

Spain never recovered from this defeat by England. It became harder for her to govern the lands she had conquered. Today only two places outside the country are still Spanish. They are the Canary Islands out in the Atlantic Ocean near the coast of Africa, and the Balearic Islands in the Mediterranean.

At the same time that Spain was losing lands she had conquered, her own lovely land tempted other countries, and the Spanish people had to endure ravaging by invading armies from England and France. The real losers during all these years of fighting were the Spanish people. They had to fight instead of growing crops, and natural resources, like forests, were neglected or used up. Spain fell farther and farther behind other countries, and even today she hasn't been able to catch up as far as she would like.

All the unhappy years of fighting in Spain were not in the long-ago past. A few years ago, in 1936, a Civil War broke out between the Spanish people who supported the elected Government, and those who, under General Francisco Franco, were opposed to the Government because it wanted to change many things that were part of the old Spanish way of life. This war went on for three whole years, and in the end, the Government lost. Franco and his army, supported by the Germans and Italians, defeated the Government forces which were helped by the Russians.

General Franco is a dictator and there are many Spanish people who disagree with the way he runs the Government and are hoping to change it. In 1947 a new constitution was written in which Franco agreed that Spain would one day have a king again, but the person who becomes king must be at least twenty-five years old. The old king is dead and there is nobody for the job now. But the king's grandson, young Prince Juan Carlos, is taking special studies so he will be ready to be king when he is old enough. And of course there are still people who would like to see Spain become a democratic republic, and not have a king at all.

In the meantime, the Spanish people and their Government

have a lot to do to make their country stable and strong again. If you were to visit Spain, you would see why the Spanish people love their country so much. You could also understand why so many different nations wanted to conquer Spain. Spain is a very beautiful country and also a country that can produce many good things. It has minerals such as iron, lead, copper and sulphur in the earth. In the south, it has a warm climate that helps to grow luscious crops of oranges, lemons, olives and grapes for wine.

You might like to take a trip from one region to another by riding on a little donkey as Spanish boys do, or in a little high-wheeled cart pulled by a donkey, the way some little Spanish girls do. Your donkey would probably not have a saddle, but just a rug or a straw mat folded across his back, and he might wear a headband of bright red and blue wool woven into a gay pattern to shade his eyes from the sun. You could carry your food and clothes for the journey in a pair of straw bags hung one on each side of your donkey's back. Along the way, you would see dozens of other little donkeys and burros. The burro is a donkey's cousin but even smaller. Donkeys and burros work with the Spanish men and boys in the fields or carry stones to help build new roads, or carry jars of water from a well to someone's house. These gentle little animals work to earn their keep in Spain.

Suppose you start your trip in the north. At the very north-westernmost tip of Spain is the region of Galicia, which everybody thought was the end of the world before Columbus showed them it wasn't. People in Galicia call themselves "Gallegos", and they live in a country of rocky sea-coasts, where the ocean pokes long fingers called "rias" back into green hills and fog rolls in almost every day. In Galicia and the neighbouring region of Asturias, fathers earn their living by fishing or by farming, and mothers make

all the clothes for their families from cloth they weave themselves. Families live in houses built from stones cleared from their own fields. This is where bagpipes are played while the young people, gaily dressed in red and green, dance their lively dances.

This northern region is quite different from the sunny south, where the climate is very hot in the summer and never really gets cold in the winter. Here in the south is Andalusia, where mountain ranges may have snow on their peaks all the year round, but down in the valleys and plains sweet-scented tropical flowers bloom in bright colours every single month. On the hillsides, grapes are grown to make wine, or silvery-green olive trees make groves against the red earth. This is a region of horses and good horsemen. Here big ranches stretch along the river banks and huge black bulls are bred.

The people of Andalusia are full of music, dancing and the love of life. They live in white houses built around courtyards full of flowers, with windows covered with designs in black wrought iron. Black-haired Andalusian women wear black lace mantillas draped over their heads, a kind of veil and shawl. They

like to carry lacy fans and wear long flashing earrings. Lots of
gypsies live in Andalusia, many of them in caves in the chalky-
white hillsides. Gypsy girls wear long red or green or blue dresses
dotted with white. They fold bright-coloured silk-fringed scarves
around their necks, and they love to wear many gold bracelets.
Andalusia is the region the Moors loved the most, so this is where
you'll see many of their lovely stone buildings full of lacelike
carvings.

It is like going into another world to journey from Andalusia into western Spain. In Extremadura, the land where the Conquistadores lived, and in León, there are great sweeping plains where the land is not very fertile because there are long dry seasons. Sheep, fruit and pigs are the main sources of making a living, and the people must work very hard. They do not have time for as much fun as the Andalusians do. These people are quiet but proud. They are especially proud of their universities, libraries and cathedrals.

Still another little world in this country of contrasts is found in the eastern part of Spain, along the Mediterranean coast and

28

in the region inland from this coast. The coastal regions are called, from north to south, Catalonia, Valencia and Murcia, all very pretty names. Catalonia has a long sea-coast which is cut by many bays and coves reaching right back into the mountains, which rise straight from the sea. Many white sand beaches, rimmed with pine trees, invite you to stop and swim and sunbathe. If you stopped, you could have fun climbing around the ruins of old walls and watchtowers on the hills looking out to sea. Once upon a time on these hills, lookouts used to give warning when pirates werc sailing up to plunder the villages. One of these Catalonian villages, called Tossa de Mar, has a whole village built inside the walls on top of a hill above the ordinary village. People used to gather in this hilltop hideout for protection against pirates. The

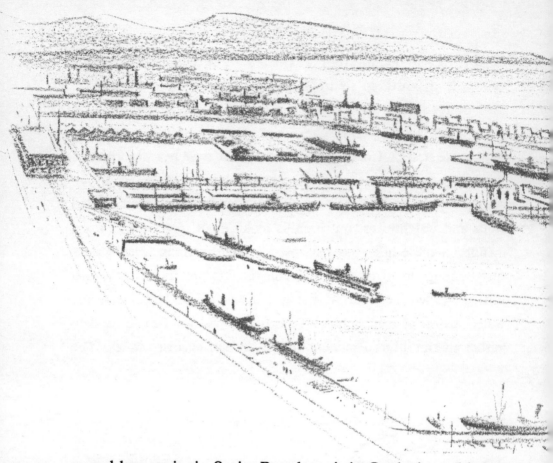

second largest city in Spain, Barcelona, is in Catalonia, and it has a very busy harbour where ships of all nations sail in and out every day.

Valencia, south of Catalonia, is a land of flowers. Carnations, roses, jasmine, scarlet bougainvillaea, vines, and orange and lemon blossoms fill the air with perfume. Every Spaniard loves flowers, and every window and courtyard is full of blossoms.

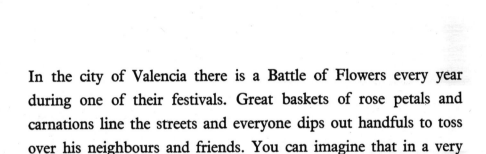

In the city of Valencia there is a Battle of Flowers every year
during one of their festivals. Great baskets of rose petals and
carnations line the streets and everyone dips out handfuls to toss
over his neighbours and friends. You can imagine that in a very
short time the whole city looks as if it were paved with flowers.

In Sitges, a small fishing village a few miles north of Valencia
where the most beautiful carnations in Spain are grown, there is a
Carnation Festival every June, and here the main square actually
*is* paved with flower petals, laid out in gorgeous designs for the
occasion. The land in the region of Valencia is so fertile that,
with the help of the irrigation system set up long ago by the Moors,
the people today grow as many as four crops a year of rice, vegetables, melons and oranges.

Murcia has a small bit of sea-coast, but the rest of it is mostly desert land where the earth looks like chalk-dust. It gets so hot people can't go out in the middle of the day. They stay indoors in the cool darkness as much as possible. Murcia is very much like North Africa, and in some of the old towns the women still wear heavy veils over their faces the way the Moors from North Africa did. You wouldn't be at all surprised to see a camel train in the chalky dust of the dry river bed, but instead, it is just another procession of little donkeys carrying goods to market in their straw saddlebags, driven by men hiding under huge hats from the burning sun.

The regions of Navarre and Aragon, in the north-east, are quite different from Murcia's desert. They have a rich, mountainous countryside with the tall Pyrenees marching across the north. Many wild animals are found in these regions, including some which are rare in other parts of the world, like the chamois, the ibex, the wild boar, bears, several kinds of deer, and the great golden eagle. Like other northern regions of Spain, there's snow in the winter and people go sledging and ski-ing.

Just to the north are the Basque Provinces, on the southern slopes of the Pyrenees and stretching along the Bay of Biscay. The Basque people are known as the "Mystery Men of Europe", because nobody is sure where they came from. Nobody knows where the strange language they speak came from either. We do know that they are a very ancient people, perhaps direct descendants of the original Iberians. The Basques are fearless and daring, and are noted throughout the world as excellent sailors and shepherds. When you visit the Basques, you will notice that they all like to eat enormous meals, they like to gamble, and they like to play "jai alai", a very fast ball game which they invented.

"Jai alai" means "happy festival" in the Basque language, and the game is a very exciting and happy one. The ball, slightly smaller than a cricket ball, is very hard and can travel very fast. Players have curved baskets attached to their right wrists, and they must scoop up or catch the ball in these baskets and immediately throw it and try to hit a certain spot marked off on the wall. If it doesn't hit the right spot, the opposing team scores a point. If it hits the right spot, the other team must try to scoop it up before it bounces and send it back, hitting a certain spot on the other side of the court.

You can see that it can be a very fast and complicated game. You would be able to see jai alai played in specially built concrete courts in many cities in Spain. A jai alai court is called a "fronton". But in the Basque country you would see all the men and boys in the village playing jai alai behind the church, using the high stone wall as their court. Girls don't play it very often, but when they do it is a very pretty sight, because they wear wide skirts of blue or red with many white petticoats underneath. When they run and turn to hit the ball, their skirts swing around wildly and make them look like spinning tops.

Completely different from the Basque country and all other regions is the central part of Spain. It is a high plateau bordered by still higher rugged rocky mountains. The weather is very hot in summer and very cold in winter, with scorching or icy winds blasting across the land because there are no forests to break their force. Great grey boulders thrust out of purple-green hillsides, and rivers cut deep gorges in the grey soil. This central part is made up of two regions, Old and New Castile. Old Castile is to the north, and cattle graze in the green fields fed by mountain streams.

Castile means "land of castles", and both Old and New Castile

have cities built around castles and cathedrals, sometimes sur-
rounded by walls built during the years of warfare. One of these
cities in Castile is Avila, which has high stone walls so thick
that four or five soldiers could march side by side on top all
the way around the city. There are 88 round towers rising from
these walls, where sentries and lookouts were posted, but only
16 ways to get in and out, so that the city could be guarded more
easily.

Not far from Avila is the famous palace of El Escorial, where
most of the kings and queens of Spain are buried. Castile isn't
the only part of Spain with castles, of course. If you were visiting
Spain today, you could stay overnight in many of these castles
and pretend you were a king or queen of lovely Spain. These
castles made into hotels are called "paradores", and a visit to one
of them is great fun.

Because Castile is in the very heart of Spain, the capital, Madrid, is located there. Madrid is a lively, bustling, modern city of more than $1\frac{1}{2}$ million people. It is the highest capital in Europe, being almost half a mile above sea level in the centre of the great mesa or tableland of Castile. Madrid is not a very old city compared with such ancient cities as Avila, but it has an old section built around the Plaza Mayor—the main square—where steps lead down into winding, narrow streets with arches and covered pavements. The larger part of Madrid is a modern city with wide boulevards lined with trees, where people can sit outside the cafés sipping coffee or wine or lemonade and watching other people streaming by.

Sometimes it seems that everybody in Madrid lives out of doors all the time, because there are so many people on the streets all day and all night. Meals are served very late—lunch is at 2 o'clock or later, and dinner not until about 10. Concerts, plays and films do not start until 11 o'clock at night, or even midnight. Even very young children and babies stay up late with their parents, to visit a pavement café with friends or to go to a cinema. Only in the middle of the day, when it is hot, everybody goes indoors for a long nap. This is called a "siesta", and during siesta time the streets of Madrid and all other Spanish cities are deserted. Shops and offices are closed. There is almost no traffic on the streets and boulevards. From 1 to 5 every afternoon, a stranger in Spain might think that a great calamity had happened and made Spain a land of sleeping princes and princesses.

After siesta, the streets wake to an even more bustling life than before. Offices and stores open again to serve their customers until 7 or 8 o'clock at night. The pavement cafés and restaurants become busier than ever. Every chair is taken, and the conversation goes on at such a fast rate that unless you understood Spanish very well, you could be lost in the rushing sound of it.

Spain has other proud cities besides Madrid. Two, whose historics go back to the days of the Moors, are Granada and Toledo.

Granada is the city in Andalusia which the Moors loved most and held longest. They fought hard to keep it, and when they finally surrendered it to Ferdinand and Isabella in 1492 they wept bitterly, for it seemed to them they had lost a Paradise. The great fortress-palace of the Moors in Granada is called the Alhambra, which means "red castle". About a hundred years ago

an American author, Washington Irving, went to live in the Alhambra. He found the romantic castle very much as the Moors had left it, except for the dust which hadn't been removed for 400 years. He walked through the echoing corridors and into the moonlit courtyards with their silent fountains. He talked with dozens of old Spanish and gypsy storytellers to learn all he could about the Alhambra. He even claimed he could see the ghosts of the sultans who had once lived there. Then he wrote a book, *Tales of the Alhambra*, which we can still read and enjoy. Because of his book, the Alhambra was cleaned and restored to all its former beauty.

Today the carved white and golden stonework of this castle shines with the splendour of long ago. One of its most interesting courtyards is called the Court of the Lions. Twelve very old stone lions, each with a different expression on his face, stand in a circle in the centre, supporting the curved bowl of a fountain on their backs. Out of each lion's mouth trickles a little stream of water, helping to cool the air. Everyone who visits the Alhambra loves these funny old lions and goes away with a picture of them.

The Moorish sultans entertained their guests and held big parties in courtyards like this one. But they lived with their families and servants in another part of the Alhambra, with

gardens and a sparkling pool where the royal ladies bathed. Looking out through certain of the arching, carved windows, the sultans could see the snow-covered Sierra Nevada Mountains. The Sierra Nevada peaks have snow all the year round, even in the hottest summers. When the Moors lived in the Alhambra, swift-running slaves would bring snow from the mountains to make sherbet for the sultans and their guests in hot weather.

From other windows in the Alhambra the sultans could see Sacro Monte—the Holy Mountain—where gypsies still live today in whitewashed caves. Many centuries ago the gypsies didn't have homes, but wandered throughout the world. When some of them came to Granada, they fell in love with the city and decided to stay. Now there are thousands of them living in Andalusia, many of them in Sacro Monte. Their cave-homes are really quite comfortable. Many have fine copper cooking pots hanging on the walls and beautiful works of art, and hangings of hand-woven fabrics. If you go to Granada, you can visit a gypsy cave and the gypsies will dance for you to a kind of music which is called "flamenco". Nobody knows where the flamenco came from, but some say it is as old as the Phoenicians, and some say—even older.

Toledo is another old, old city in Spain—at one time the capital. Toledo is built on a series of hills above a river, called

Tagus, which winds around the base of the city like a natural moat around a fortress. Nearly four hundred years ago a Greek painter came to Toledo and stayed to become one of Spain's — and the world's — greatest artists. He was known as "El Greco", which means The Greek, and today most people have forgotten his real name.

Perhaps you have seen his famous painting of the city he loved, called "View of Toledo". If you have, you know what Toledo looks like today, for it has changed very little since El Greco painted it. You could take your crayons or paints to the same spot across the River Tagus where he stood with his canvas and easel, and you would see the same rapids in the river, the same arched gateways in the city walls, the same cathedral spire rising from a hill.

Then you could cross an old bridge, and go through a Moorish gateway into the town. Walking along a cobble-stone street, you might pass an old church which has iron chains hanging on its walls. These are the chains of Christian slaves captured by Moors, then freed by Christian armies.

At the top of one hill you would discover an old house with red tiled roof and a garden full of roses, geraniums, mimosa, jasmine and oleanders. This is the house where El Greco lived, and you would see his easel, his bedroom, his kitchen and furniture just as he left them. In a small museum next to the house you would find paintings by El Greco, mostly pictures of saints and portraits of famous Spaniards of his time. One of his paintings is in a chapel in the town and others are in other churches throughout Spain, and in the Prado Museum in Madrid, along with those of other great Spanish painters like Velasquez, Goya and Murillo.

The people of Toledo have a special art of their own—making fine jewellery called "Toledo ware". The Moors brought the knack from the ancient city of Damascus. Threads of gold and silver are woven into intricate patterns with fine steel. When the piece is put into a hot furnace, the steel part of the pattern turns black, then the gold and silver designs are polished until they shine. Originally the Moors made their big swords this way, but today Toledo ware is bracelets, earrings, cuff links and other small jewellery.

The people of Toledo also make glistening glazed tiles. Some of these show scenes from the lives of favourite Spanish heroes, real and imaginary. There are some Toledo tiles that will tell you about Don Quixote of La Mancha, a hero invented 350 years ago by Miguel de Cervantes.

Cervantes wanted to tease his fellow countrymen about reading so many books with stories that could never happen in real life.

So he wrote a book of his own about Don Quixote, a foolish old fellow who imagined he was a handsome knight. The poor Don rode all around the country on a rickety old horse dreaming he was rescuing beautiful ladies and fighting imaginary battles for

his king. Once he even tried to fight a windmill, thinking it was a giant! Another time he thought a shepherd and his flock were an army!

Cervantes' fun-poking book is still read and laughed over by people throughout the whole world. Today, if you were to drive from Granada to Toledo or Madrid, you would pass through Don Quixote's country, La Mancha, and you would see windmills and the shepherds leading their sheep and goats, with all the countryside looking much as Cervantes described it through Don Quixote's eyes.

Wherever you stopped for the night, at 7 o'clock in the evening you would see people walking along. Every family comes out to join in this evening custom which is called "paseo". Of course the children come too, dressed in their best clothes. But boys and girls do not walk together. Two or three girls will walk by, arm-in-arm, and several boys will walk by, talking together and looking at the girls from the corners of their eyes. In the smaller places, all the older boys walk together in one direction while all the older girls walk arm-in-arm in the opposite direction, or else on the other side of the street.

Just as boys and girls don't walk together in the paseo, they don't often play games together either—at least not after they are old enough to go to school. Before school days start, all children play singing and dancing games something like our "London Bridge". They play tag and a favourite game called "Hit the Pot". They put a tin can or an old clay pot on the end of a long stick and blindfold the child who is "It". The others then run around with the stick while "It" tries to knock off the can with another stick. But when they are six years old, all little boys and girls must go to school, and—except in small villages where there are only a few children to study with one teacher—they go to separate schools, so they stop playing together then, too.

Little girls skip and play with jacks and dolls. Or they play singing games which act out the parts of kings and queens and princesses. Little boys are most interested in games with balls, like jai alai or football.

The favourite game of most little boys in Spain is "Torero". In this game they pretend they are bullfighters, who are called "toreros". Every boy in Spain dreams of growing up to be the greatest bullfighter in the world. Bullfighting is one of the most exciting things in life to every Spaniard.

45

Every big city has a great bullring, a round building with many tiers of seats and no roof, called the "Plaza de Toros". "Toro" is the bull. The bulls are especially bred for the ring, because no ordinary cow or bull would be able to take part in this colourful pageant. Almost every Sunday afternoon throughout the year, and at holiday times, there is a "corrida" or bullfight, and everybody goes to see the toreros fight the bulls.

Bullfighters in Spain are the same heroes to Spanish boys and girls that famous cricketers are to British youngsters. This is the reason why you'll see all the little Spanish boys playing Torero. One pretends he is the toro and wears a basket over his head as he charges at the one pretending he is the torero with a red cape and wooden sword.

Although Spanish children like to play, they are also very serious about school-work, because they know that if Spain is to be a wise member of the family of nations, she needs educated citizens. During the Civil War it was very hard for young people to get an education, and some of the schools and universities were destroyed by bombs or fires. Now the universities have been rebuilt, and more schools are being built every year.

Some boys and girls go to Catholic church schools, and they are taught by priests and nuns. According to law, everyone must go to school until the age of fourteen. Then, if the family can

afford it, they can go on to higher schools and the university. If the family is poor but a boy is very bright, he may win a scholarship by getting high marks. Because boys are more likely than girls to go to a university, they study more science and mathematics at school than their sisters do. Of course they all study reading, writing, history, arithmetic and good manners.

When a Spanish boy grows up and has a university education, he may become a doctor, lawyer, banker, newspaperman or government worker, just as any of you may. If he is going to be a farmer, a fisherman, or fashion things with his hands as a carpenter or wrought-iron maker does, he probably won't go to school after he is fourteen. If he is going to do the same thing as his father does, his father will teach him. Otherwise, he may become an apprentice, which means that he will work alongside grown-ups who already do what he wants to learn. He learns by doing it with them.

Little Spanish girls, who wear pinafores to school and do their hair in pigtails, are more interested in learning how to be good mothers, because every little Spanish girl dreams of marrying and having lots of children. They learn how to read and write, and the history of their country, but they also learn how to cook and sew and bring up children.

Recently some Spanish girls have started learning how to be lawyers, doctors and teachers. These girls, like their brothers, go on to universities. Some girls also learn shorthand and typing so that they can work in offices. Before the Civil War there were no girls in offices, but today they like being secretaries and typists just as girls in Britain do. Still, even these modern Spanish girls don't have the freedom to go to parties or out with boys, the way British girls do, unless they are engaged to be married. When they go out at night for the paseo or to attend the theatre or a cinema, they go with other girls or with their whole family.

A strong family bond unites all Spanish people. Fathers and mothers and children spend as much time together as they possibly can. If being together means that children must go with parents into the fields at harvest time, then they go, even if they only play around and don't really help. In the evenings when the father and mother go to the paseo or sit in a café to talk with their friends, their children go with them.

Always the whole family goes to church together. One of the most important days in a Spanish child's life is the day of confirmation. Then the family and relatives and friends from miles around come to celebrate. All over Spain, on a Sunday morning, you'll see the little girls in their long white dresses with white gloves and veils, looking proud and happy as they walk to church with their beaming mothers and fathers for their confirmation.

When boys are confirmed they wear white suits, with a cape lined in scarlet or blue satin and trimmed with gold braid. If the family has enough money, they may hire a horse-drawn carriage. The driver wears a tall black stovepipe silk hat and the carriage doors and horses' bridles are decorated with white flowers.

The Catholic Church is very important in Spanish life. The Apostle James came to preach in Spain, and later, after he had been killed in Palestine, his body was brought back to Spain for burial. His tomb is in the beautiful Cathedral of Santiago—which is the way Spanish people say St. James—in Compostela, in northern Spain. For thousands of years people from all over the world have come as pilgrims to Compostela. Many little Spanish boys are named Santiago, or perhaps Jaime, another way to say James in Spanish, for Santiago is the patron saint of all Spain.

Every city and village also has its very own private patron saint. Once a year there is a village festival or "fiesta" in his or her honour. If you were to travel through Spain you would find a fiesta somewhere every day of the year! These fiestas start in the morning when all the people go to church, which is always decorated with hundreds of flowers and candles. Then in the

afternoon or evening there is a long parade from the church
through the main streets and back to the church again, with the
figure of the saint standing on a flower-draped platform which is
carried on the shoulders of young men.

Choirs sing, candles and incense burn, and all the people stand
in reverence along the route. A bullfight is usually a feature of a
saint's day too, with the whole town going to the Plaza de Toros
to watch. The paseo will be especially gay at fiesta time, and as
darkness falls, the guitars will start to twang, castanets will click
and all the young people will gather in the main square to take

part in folk dances until morning. Sometimes the saint's fiesta will last a whole week, with bullfights every afternoon and a fair every night.

One of the most unusual fiestas in all Spain is held every March in Valencia in honour of St. Joseph. It is called the "Fallas de San José" because of the huge, grotesque figures called "fallas" which are the main feature of the celebration. Every club and religious group in the city spends weeks in advance of St. Joseph's Day building these figures out of papier mâché, and each group tries to keep its design secret until the fiesta takes place. The best falla wins a prize, and at the end of the three-day celebration, all the fallas except the prize-winner are burned in a big bonfire while the people dance around it and fireworks are shot into the sky.

Of all holidays, Christmas is one of the merriest in Spanish homes. "Noche Buena", or Christmas Eve, is a time for families to sit down to a wonderful feast. The mothers and older sisters of the family have been preparing this feast for months, and fathers have been collecting the best Spanish wines to store away until now. Turkey is the traditional dish at Spanish Christmas dinners just as it is here. And Christmas is one of the few times turkey is ever served in most Spanish homes, so it is really a special treat.

Spicy hams, stuffed roast lamb, and special fish dishes are also served with the roast turkey. And no Christmas table would be complete without "turrones"—a sweet made of honey and almonds, something like our nougat. Dried figs and grapes, walnuts and hazelnuts load the table even more. After dinner, the family goes to midnight services at church called "Misa de Gallo"; then they come home and celebrate until morning.

There are no Christmas trees in Spain, but each family makes its own Nativity scene, which is set out in time for Christmas Eve. In some cities contests are held for the most beautiful "Belen" scenes, as they are called, because "Belen" is the way Spanish people say Bethlehem. On Christmas Day everybody goes calling to see the Belens in other people's houses.

Sometimes grown-ups exchange gifts on Christmas Day, but Spanish children do not receive their gifts until January 6, Three Kings' Day. Instead of Santa Claus, the Three Wise Men, Melchior, Caspar and Balthasar leave gifts in the children's shoes. The shoes are set out in a window or near the fireplace, filled with hay so the camels of the Three Kings may feast. In the morning the hay is gone and toys, nuts, fruit and sweets have taken its place.

Holy Week, the week starting with Palm Sunday and ending
with Easter, is another important time in Spanish life. On Palm
Sunday, everyone throughout the country has palm branches from
Elche, an old town where the only palm grove in Europe grows.

After carrying the branches in processions through the streets and into the churches and cathedrals, people hang them on the balconies of their houses, where they remain until the fresh palm branches of the next year replace them.

The most colourful celebration of Holy Week is held in Seville, a city in sunny Andalusia. Every night there are processions of robed and hooded men moving silently through streets lined with thousands of men, women and children. All the figures of saints and Madonnas from all the churches and the Cathedral are carried in one procession or another. The figures are dressed in costly vestments and jewels, and the procession is lighted by flickering torches and candles. As the figures pass beneath balconies crowded with watchers, a singer will suddenly break into a spontaneous, unaccompanied song, called a "saeta", to salute the saint being carried by. The saeta is the same sort of song the Moors used to sing when they lived in Seville and other cities in Andalusia, and today it is usually sung by gypsies, thousands of whom live here.

Night after night these processions go on, until Good Friday, when the most gorgeous one of all starts at 3 o'clock in the morning. This is the procession of the Virgin of Macarena, the patron of bullfighters and all Seville. The Virgin is dressed up in robes of silver and gold and wears jewels given by famous bullfighters and wealthy people. The men who march in this procession wear costumes of rich red and gold, and there is a guard of honour dressed like ancient Roman centurions. The "Macarena" is the most popular patron of Seville, and everyone watches her procession until it takes her back to her shrine in the gypsy section, Triana, followed by thousands of gaily clad gypsies who spend the rest of the night singing and dancing to the throbbing of guitars.

Shortly after Holy Week, Seville has another gay festival, this time called a "feria", which is rather like a big country fair. For two weeks everybody celebrates all day and all night, singing and dancing and visiting friends for a glass of wine. Every day there is a bullfight, and at night there are concerts, dance and art shows, and plays. The huge fair grounds blaze with light, and ferris wheels and merry-go-rounds spin gaily round and round.

Once upon a time, the feria was an auction for horses and cattle, and today it is still a time when the best horsemen show off their fine horses and their skill at riding. During the feria, the proud horsemen wear leather aprons something like cowboys' chaps over their tight grey trousers. Their bolero jackets are black trimmed with braid, and their hats are black too, the flat, wide-brimmed felt hats which horsemen always wear in Spain.

Horses are groomed until they shine, and flowers and ribbons are twined in their manes and tails and decorate their bridles. Beautiful black-haired girls dress up like gypsies, something they would not be allowed to do at any other time. As the girls ride in the saddles behind their young men, the long, flounced, polka-dotted skirts of red, green or blue fall down over the horse's side. Black lace mantillas are draped over very tall combs in their hair, and a gay flower is usually pinned behind one ear. Every carriage, every farm cart, every house and every person is decorated with flowers.

At harvest time, when olives, grapes, fruit or grain are brought in from the land, there is much merry-making, too. At Jerez de la Frontera, a sunny town in Andalusia where everybody works at growing grapes and making them into a famous wine called sherry, the harvest festival comes just before the grapes are ready to be harvested, in September.

High-wheeled vineyard carts decorated with vines and flowers are pulled, by sturdy oxen, out of every vineyard in the countryside, carrying

57

all the pretty girls who work there and a basket of new grapes. The carts wind through the streets to the Cathedral, where the grapes are blessed and all the people pray and give thanks for a good harvest. Then, in the square in front of the Cathedral, a great flock of pigeons is let loose into the air. These are homing pigeons, and they fly back to their homes in every part of Spain, carrying the message that the harvest is about to begin. There is dancing in the streets all night, and the next day there are bull-fights, races and more dancing. Then the people all go to work to harvest the grapes.

On Spanish holidays, there is plenty to eat and drink. For visitors, eating is fun even on any ordinary day. If you were to travel from region to region in Spain, you would notice that people eat different foods in different places. Along the sea-coasts, of course, they eat many kinds of fish. In the north, one of the

favourite fish dishes is made of codfish cooked in a delicious sauce
of red and green peppers flavoured with garlic. In Valencia you

would eat "paella" made of many kinds of shellfish, chicken, ham and rice flavoured with saffron, a yellow spice which grows in Spain. Paella is made in a big round iron pan over a charcoal fire, and the mussels, shrimps, pieces of chicken and everything else that makes it good are tossed in, a handful at a time, until the whole dish is ready to be served straight from the pan it was cooked in.

Most families have a big lunch, at about 2 o'clock. If the weather is cool, this is very likely to be a pot of stew, or "cocido". Depending on what part of the country you are in, this cocido might be made of fish, lamb, beef or chicken. Whatever the meat or fish may be, the cocido also includes all the vegetables that grow in the garden at that time of year. It is apt to be flavoured with garlic, sweet Spanish red peppers, and perhaps several spoonfuls of sherry.

In the hot summer weather in Andalusia, people eat a delicious cold soup as their main dish at lunch, and sometimes at dinner too. This soup is called "gazpacho", and it is made with Spanish olive oil, vinegar, tomato juice and ice water. Very fine bread crumbs help to make it thick, and little pieces of fresh, cold tomatoes, cucumbers, green peppers, olives and onions float on top.

Everybody in Spain eats a great many "churros". Churros are something like doughnuts, but they are twisted into odd shapes and fried in olive oil until they are crisp all the way through, not just on the outside. They are very fine for breakfast with hot chocolate, and they are also good with sugar sprinkled on them as a between-meals snack. Another snack is almonds, grown in Spain, and shrimps the size of your little finger.

Some of the foods the Spanish children eat are the same as their great-great-great-grandfathers and mothers ate, too. Mostly, the houses where they live are also very old—as old as the holiday customs that haven't changed in hundreds of years. These old ways and scenes are some of the reasons why Spain has been called "the land where time stands still".

Only now is this old Spain about to become modern Spain. New roads, railways and airfields are being built to help people get around the country faster and to send food from farms and sea-coasts to markets in a hurry. All over Spain you hear the sound of hammers and chisels, busily building a new life for the people.

Spain has joined the United Nations, and Spanish boys and girls are eager to join all boys and girls who want their countries to be partners in progress. If, in getting to know Spain, you have learned to like it, perhaps you will want to say "hello" and "good luck" to your Spanish friends. Here is how to say it: "Saludos, amigos!"

# History

Before 200 B.C.—Earliest people lived in caves in northern Spain; were conquered by Iberians, then Celts. Phoenicians and Greeks came, and finally all were conquered by Carthaginians.

201 B.C.—Romans conquered Carthaginians, began a rule lasting more than 500 years.

A.D. 406—Barbarians, especially Visigoths, came into Spain from central Europe and eventually drove out the Romans.

A.D. 711—The Moors came from North Africa and conquered all Spain in less than 10 years. Although the Christian Spaniards started fighting almost immediately for the "Reconquest" of Spain, the Moors were masters for almost 800 years.

January 2, 1492—The Reconquest of Spain was completed when the armies of Ferdinand and Isabella drove the Moors out of the Alhambra in Granada, their last stronghold.

August, 1492—Columbus sailed with his three ships from Palos in an effort to reach the Far East by sailing west; on October 12, he made his first landfall in the New World and claimed it for Spain.

1492–1588—The Golden Age of Spain. Columbus discovered more lands in the New World, and Conquistadores planted the Spanish flag all through North and South America. Spain controlled much of Europe. It was a time of great artists and writers like Velasquez, El Greco, Murillo, Lope de Vega and Cervantes.

1588—Spain's great naval Armada was defeated by England and the power of Spain began to decline throughout the world. Last overseas possessions were lost at the end of the Spanish–American War in 1898.

1931—King Alfonso XIII abdicated from his throne, went into exile; Spain became a republic.

1936–1939—The Spanish Civil War. Nationalists led by General Francisco Franco won the war and Franco became Chief of State.

1947—The Law of Succession was adopted by Spanish Parliament, providing for a future King and new Spanish monarchy; this law altered in 1956 so that the monarchy may be established sooner than originally planned.

1956—Spain admitted to the United Nations.

# Index